About South West
Wales

Published by Graffeg
First published 2007
Copyright © Graffeg 2007
ISBN 978 1 905582 06 8

Graffeg, Radnor Court, 256 Cowbridge
Road East, Cardiff CF5 1GZ Wales UK.
Tel: +44(0)29 2037 7312
sales@graffeg.com www.graffeg.com
Graffeg are hereby identified as the
authors of this work in accordance
with section 77 of the Copyrights,
Designs and Patents Act 1988.

Distributed by the Welsh Books
Council www.cllc.org.uk
castellbrychan@cllc.org.uk

A CIP Catalogue record for this book
is available from the British Library.

Designed and produced by
Peter Gill & Associates
sales@petergill.com
www.petergill.com

Map base information reproduced
by permission of Ordnance Survey
on behalf of HMSO
© Crown Copyright.
All rights reserved. Ordnance Survey
Licence number 100020518

About South West Wales
Written by David Williams,
foreword by Siân Lloyd

The publishers are also grateful to
the Welsh Books Council for their
financial support and marketing
advice. www.gwales.com

Every effort has been made to
ensure that the information in this
book is current and it is given in good
faith at the time of publication. Please
be aware that circumstances can
change and be sure to check details
before making travel plans.

Front cover image: Tenby Harbour.

About South West
Wales

Foreword

"Whether you live here or are visiting for the first time, I hope that this book will inspire you to explore Wales's many cultural and historical treasures, leading you to new and exciting experiences.
It is intended to be a source book of ideas for things to do."

Wales is a remarkable part of the world where, over many centuries, people have created a rich and fascinating heritage. From battle-worn castles to settled towns and villages, from mines and quarries to elegant historic houses, there are tremendous places to visit.

Museums draw upon wonderful original material to tell our story. Many towns have local-history museums. The National Museum Wales, an impressive group of museums and galleries, illuminates our collective past through informative and innovative displays.

Our enthusiasm for culture, especially music and literature, is famous. Wales produces stars of concert hall, opera, stage, screen and rock arena – along with gifted writers and poets. There is strength in depth, from keen amateur activity in local halls and eisteddfodau to the thriving professional sphere. Major festivals, and smaller events, accommodate every cultural and artistic activity: music, literature, theatre, dance, the visual arts and others.

Wales asserts its cultural individuality in an increasingly interconnected and globalised world. The long history of the Welsh people has evolved into a forward-looking modern identity, based on respect for the past. As someone who works in both England and Wales, and travels widely, I enjoy sharing this distinctive sense of identity with people I meet.

I am fluently bilingual in Welsh and English and thank my parents for sending me to a Welsh school. The opportunities I received there – especially in public speaking, drama and music – set me on course to become a broadcaster.

The Welsh language, spoken by around half a million people, supports a wonderful literature and a thriving culture. English and Welsh enjoy official status together and many other languages are heard too, especially in the multicultural cities of Cardiff, Swansea and Newport.

Whether you live here or are visiting for the first time, I hope that this book will inspire you to explore Wales's many cultural and historic treasures. It is intended to be a source book of ideas for things to do. So, please enjoy the evocative photographs and learn interesting things but, above all, be sure to get out and about to experience the wonders of Wales for yourself.

Siân Lloyd

Left: **St David's Cathedral.** Built upon the site of St David's 6th-century monastery, St David's Cathedral has been a place of pilgrimage and worship for many hundreds of years.

Introduction

This book celebrates the historical and cultural attractions that make south-west Wales such a special place. We hope that it will lead you to enjoyable discoveries and a deeper appreciation of this ancient and profoundly fascinating region and its people.

Located on the western side of the UK, Wales is bounded by the sea on three sides and shares a border with England to the east. Almost a quarter of its area enjoys special environmental designation.

Our three national parks – Snowdonia, the Brecon Beacons and the Pembrokeshire Coast – contain landscapes and habitats of international importance. Other regions throughout Wales are designated Areas of Outstanding Natural Beauty and there are more than 1,000 Sites of Special Scientific Interest.

But it is the way in which people have left their mark – on the landscape, in towns and cities, and on the world – that gives Wales its unique character. It is a place where a sense of history, and the achievements of the past, are valued by an advanced modern nation.

Wales is part of the United Kingdom and therefore is not fully a nation state. But its people certainly see themselves as a distinct nation. The Welsh language reinforces this identity, yet many people who do not speak it are also quick to assert their Welshness. The devolution of significant powers from Parliament in London to the National Assembly for Wales in Cardiff has given us one of the world's newest democratic institutions and greater autonomy.

Evidence of how people lived and worked over the centuries is preserved at our many ancient monuments, castles, historic houses and industrial locations. Wales has two UNESCO World Heritage Sites: the great medieval castles and town walls of north-west Wales and the industrial landscape of Blaenavon in the south-east.

Many places are in the care of either the National Trust or CADW, the Welsh Assembly Government's historic environment division. Museums and galleries, including the National Museum Wales, tell of our remarkable past.

The Welsh are seen as musically and lyrically gifted people. Ability in the areas is celebrated at local events and major festivals. The vigorous cultural life reflects the varied origins of the people (especially in the cities) and their typically open-minded gregariousness.

This book celebrates some of the historical and cultural attractions that make south-west Wales such a special place. We hope that it will lead you to enjoyable discoveries and a deeper appreciation of this ancient and profoundly fascinating region and its people.

David Williams

Left: **National Eisteddfod. Held at the beginning of August, the National Eisteddfod moves to a different part of Wales each year.**

7

About this book

The aim of this book is to give you a taste of some of the main cultural and historical attractions of south-west Wales. It is one of a series of four regional pocket guides that cover, between them, the whole of Wales.

You will find information on many locations to visit and events to enjoy: castles, historic houses, industrial-heritage sites, museums, galleries, large festivals and local gatherings.

Each entry provides guidance on how to get there. Maps show the towns and villages mentioned, and the main roads. Contact information and website addresses will enable you to find current event programmes, opening times and any admission charges, and to plan your visit in detail.

We list the best-known attractions but, of course, Wales has such a rich heritage that there are many more places to explore. The main tourism websites – and those of organisations including CADW and the National Trust – are included here.

We also provide details of Tourism Information Centres, places to stay and eat, advice on south-west Wales's public transport system and an introduction to the Welsh language. The book concludes with an index of places, attractions, festivals and events.

We hope you enjoy browsing in search of interesting places to visit and things to do.

South West Wales
From the dramatic coast of Pembrokeshire to the exciting city of Swansea, this south-western corner of Wales is a great place to visit.

Above left: **Pembroke Castle.** Once the seat of major barons, Pembroke Castle is the birth place of Henry Tudor – father of Henry VIII and grandfather of Elizabeth I.
Above right: **The Boathouse at Laugharne.** Dylan Thomas spent the last four years of his life at the Boathouse and wrote a number of his major works here including *Under Milk Wood*. It is now a centre devoted to his life and works.

Contents

Welcome to South West Wales with a
spectacular coastline extending from
Pembrokeshire (the only coast in
England and Wales to be designated a
national park) to Swansea Bay. Gower
peninsula is an Area of Outstanding
Natural Beauty. Explore Swansea,
Wales's 'city by the sea', and discover
the wonderful countryside and
gardens of Carmarthenshire.

Cardigan Bay

Aberporth

A487

B4333

Cardigan

A484

Newcas
Emlyn

Cilgerran

A487

Cenarth

Felindre

B4332

B4332

Rosslare

B4333

Fishguard

Pembrokeshire
Coast National
Park

Pontfaen

Preseli Hills

B4332

A487

A40

A478

Abercastle

Porthgain

Abereiddi

A487

B4329

B429

B4313

St David's

Porthclais

Solva

Treffgarne

Upper Scolton

Nolton Haven

Keeston

A487

St Brides Bay

Haverfordwest

A40

Narberth

Whitland

St Clears

Pembrokeshire
Coast National
Park

A4076

A4075

A477

Laugharne

Llansteffa

Milford Haven

Kilgetty

Pendine

Pembroke Dock

Rosslare

Carmarthen Bay

Pembroke

A4139

Tenby

Lamphey

St Govan's

B4319

Caldey Island

N

Scale
Kilometres
0 2 4 6 8 10
0 1 2 3 4 5 6
Miles

Key

National Park

South West Wales

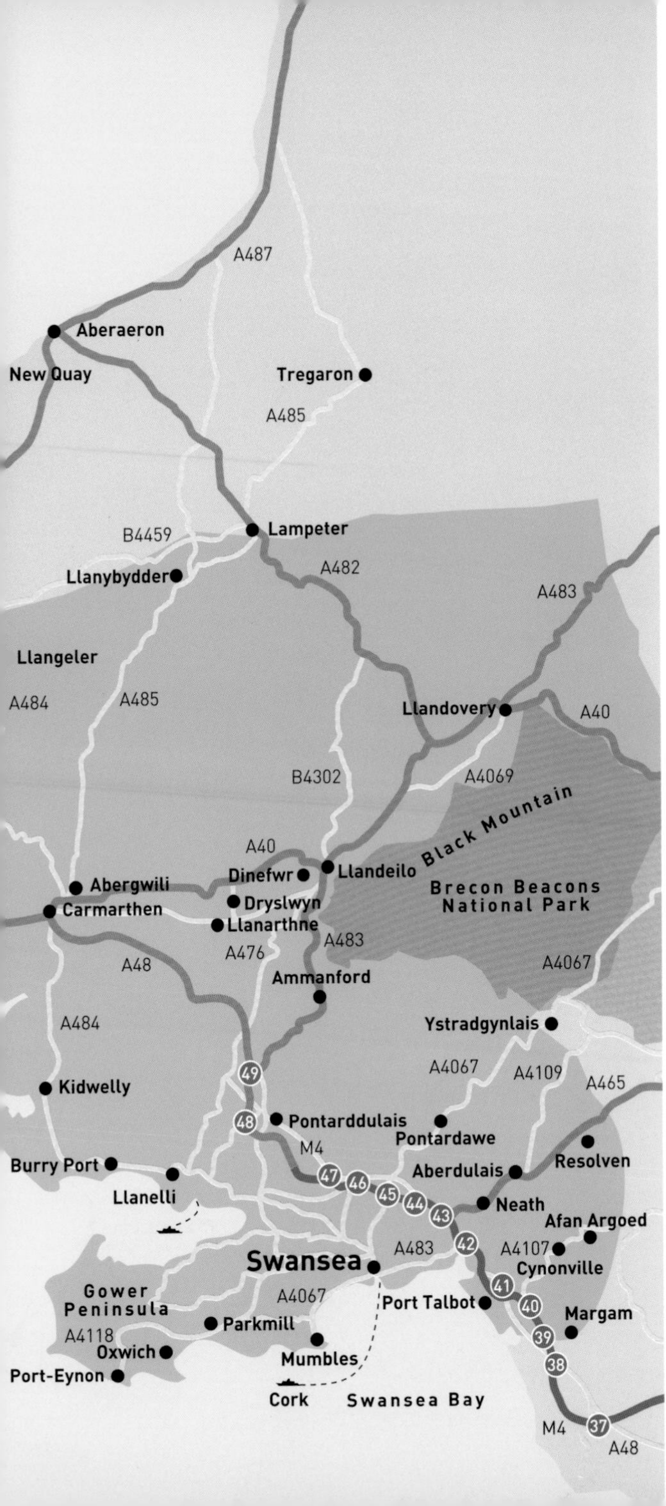

A487

Aberaeron
New Quay

Tregaron

A485

B4459   Lampeter
Llanybydder   A482

A483

Llangeler

A484   A485   Llandovery   A40

B4302   A4069

Black Mountain

A40
Dinefwr   Llandeilo   Brecon Beacons
Abergwili   Dryslwyn   National Park
Carmarthen   Llanarthne
A476   A483
A48   Ammanford   A4067

A484   Ystradgynlais

A4067   A4109   A465

Kidwelly

49
48   Pontarddulais
Burry Port   M4   Pontardawe
Llanelli   47 46 45   Aberdulais   Resolven
44 43   Neath
Afan Argoed
Swansea   A483   42   A4107
Cynonville
Gower   A4067   Port Talbot   41
Peninsula   40   Margam
A4118   Parkmill   39
Oxwich   Mumbles   38
Port-Eynon   Cork   Swansea Bay
M4   37
A48

Pembrokeshire

Ancient monuments and historic harbours abound in this long-populated region. Explore St David's Cathedral, the Landsker line, Milford Haven, Haverfordwest, Solva, Tenby, the Preseli Hills, Pentre Ifan, Caldey Island and Castell Henllys.

Castles. Pembrokeshire is dotted with many castles, large and small. The powerful keep of the imposing castle in **Pembroke** speaks of the bitter conflict between the Welsh and the Normans. Delightful **Carew**, with its tidal mill, illustrates the transition from stronghold to country house; one of the finest Celtic crosses in Wales stands nearby. **Manorbier** was the birthplace of traveller and scholar-cleric Gerald of Wales. **Picton Castle** has been in the hands of the same family since the 15th century and houses fine furniture and an art gallery. But it was the series of small castles along the **Landsker line**, between **Llawhaden** and **St David's**, that

defined the character of the county. The region to the south of the line, including the ports of **Milford Haven** and **Tenby**, was occupied in medieval times by English settlers and their Flemish allies and came to be known as "the little England beyond Wales".
• www.visitpembrokeshire.com

Above left: **Pembroke Castle.**
The intimidating central tower, and the natural moat provided by the estuary, would have made any attacker think twice.
Above right: **Ceibwr area.** Some six miles (9km) from its northern end, the Pembrokeshire Coast Path passes the small port of Ceibwr and follows high cliffs above caves and a natural arch.

The Pembrokeshire Coast Path.
A 179-mile (288km) national trail around the south-western peninsula of Wales – the only stretch of coastline in England and Wales to be designated a National Park. As well as being outstandingly scenic, this coast abounds in prehistoric monuments, industrial heritage sites and fascinating seaports. The path passes close to Tenby, Pembroke, Milford Haven, Solva, St David's and Fishguard.
• The path links St Dogmael's, near Cardigan, and Amroth in the south of the county – the official National Trail Guide is widely available from bookshops and tourist information centres.

Caldey Island

A pleasant boat trip from Tenby will take you to Caldey Island, where you may explore the **Old Priory** and the medieval churches of **St David** and **St Illtyd**, and are welcome to join the monks at one of their chanted services in the Abbey Church. **Caldey Abbey** was originally built in 1910 by Anglican Benedictine monks, though it later became a Cistercian community. It was designed in Italianate style by Penarth-based architect John Coates-Carter and is now a listed building. The monks are famous for making perfumes, chocolate and shortbread, which are sold in the village. **The Post Office** is also a museum giving an insight into

the island's history. There are also some marvellous walks on the island.
• There are regular boat services from Tenby during the holiday season. Phone: 01834 844453 www.caldey-island.co.uk

Cardigan

Cilgerran Castle. The time-worn towers of Cilgerran rise majestically above woodland on the rim of the deep Teifi gorge. Originally one of the strongholds of the Welsh region of Deheubarth, it was extended by the Norman baron William Marshall. He added the powerful towers and thick curtain wall that so inspired JMW Turner and the many Victorian travellers who came upriver by boat from Cardigan to savour its romance.
• South of Cardigan, off the A478. Phone: 01239 621339 www.cadw.wales.gov.uk

Castell Henllys reconstructed Iron Age settlement.
This scheduled ancient monument is an Iron Age hill fort dating from around 600 BC. A great deal of information about its origins has been discovered by archaeologists and you can learn all about their current

Left: **Caldey Abbey.** The monks of Caldey Island combine a spiritual lifestyle with sound business acumen as they promote their popular products locally, by mail order and on the internet.

excavations. Thatched buildings have been reconstructed on their original foundations: the chieftain's house, the granary and the smithy may all be seen in authentic guise. A sculpture trail depicts Celtic myths and legends, and there is a farm with ancient breeds of livestock.
• Near Eglwyswrw, on the A487 south-west of Cardigan.
Phone: 01239 891319
www.castellhenllys.com

Fishguard

Long established as a ferry port for Ireland, Fishguard combines a bustling town centre with the peace and quiet of the Lower Harbour, with its old stone quay and picturesque buildings.

It was just along the coast, at **Carregwastad Point**, that the last invasion force to land in Britain came ashore in 1797. A rag-tag army of around a thousand untrained French troops, mostly convicts released for the task, led by the disaffected Irish-American William Tate, attempted to raise support for a French invasion of Ireland. They

Left: **Cilgerran Castle.** With its stout defences and elevated position, Cilgerran Castle enabled its occupants to dominate the Teifi valley.
Above: **Fishguard Harbour.** The English name Fishguard comes from the Norse *fiskigadr*, meaning 'an enclosure for catching fish', and shows that the Vikings knew of this place.

were met by the sight of lines of people along the cliff-tops, including women in traditional red shawls and tall hats, who gave a good impression of a large garrison of soldiers. By the time the actual militia arrived, the French had been persuaded of the folly of their mission by, amongst others, the formidable blacksmith and cobbler Jemima Nicholas and her pitchfork. The story is told at the **Royal Oak pub**, where the surrender was accepted.

• The A40 and A487 converge on Fishguard, but consider also the scenic approach along the B4313. www.abergwaun.com

Melin Tregwynt Woollen Mill.
This beautiful whitewashed mill, owned by the same family since 1912, is located in a remote wooded valley off the A487 between Fishguard and St David's. As far back as the 17th century, local farmers used to bring their fleeces here to be spun into yarn and woven into blankets for their families. The mill continues to use traditional methods to produce blankets, spreads and throws of the highest quality, but with a fresh approach to design and colour. You can watch the weaving on weekdays throughout the year and the shop sells a wide selection of Melin Tregwynt products.

• Signed down minor roads to the coast, some four miles south-west of Fishguard.

Phone: 01348 891644
www.melintregwynt.co.uk

....

Haverfordwest

Remarkably, for somewhere so far from the sea, Haverfordwest grew as a port to serve the Norman castle and the town that grew around it from the 12th century onwards. But it was the Flemish immigrants into southern Pembrokeshire who, a couple of centuries later, developed the town into an important centre for wool, leather, dairy produce and brewing, and who exported the fruits of their energetic labour from the river quayside. The upper reaches of the Cleddau estuary had several small ports – Landshipping and Lawrenny amongst them – from which the hard coal mined in the area was transported.

• The town is easily accessible via the A40.

Haverfordwest Town Museum.
The history of the castle and town of Haverfordwest, county town of Pembrokeshire for almost a thousand years, is on display here, illuminated by intriguing exhibits and a multimedia presentation. The museum is adjacent to the early-12th century castle, which dominates the

Right: **Royal Oak pub.** Pop into the Royal Oak pub in Fishguard to learn all about the last time an invasion force landed on the British mainland.

LAST INVASION OF
BRITAIN PEACE TREATY
WAS SIGNED HERE
IN 1797

skyline of the town. Only the shell remains, but the old prison and police station inside the walls house the county archives.
• There is parking space around the town, which is a good place to explore on foot.
Phone: 01437 763087
www.haverfordwest-town-museum.org.uk

Nant y Coy Mill, Treffgarne Gorge. This restored 14th century corn mill sits in a picturesque setting below **Great Treffgarne rocks**, near Haverfordwest.
A nature trail runs alongside the stream that powers the mill. You will also find a small museum, a craft shop and a tea room.
• Five miles north of Haverfordwest, on the A40 towards Fishguard.
Phone: 01437 741671

Nolton Haven. The attractive village of Nolton Haven is typical of the many places in Pembrokeshire where you will find plenty to do. It has a popular riding centre and a quaint schoolroom, which is the venue for art exhibitions during the summer months. Traditional Welsh food and entertainment enliven the audiences at Celtic Corner.
• Take the A487 from Haverfordwest to Simpson Cross, then narrow lanes to the village.

Pembrokeshire Motor Museum. At Keeston Hill, near Haverfordwest, you will find on display an interesting range of locally owned veteran, vintage and classic cars, motorcycles and

bikes. There is often work going on in the restoration workshop and the staff will be pleased to explain the intricacies of the fine vehicles in their care.
• About three miles north-west of Haverfordwest, on the A487 towards St David's.
Phone: 01437 710950
www.pembsmotormuseum.co.uk

Scolton Manor House and Country Park.

You gain a strong impression of the daily life of the occupants of this Victorian manor from its "upstairs, downstairs" exhibits and historical artefacts.
The surrounding country park has an ecological theme and hosts numerous events in the summer: its attractions include a steam train, smithy and

wheelwright's workshop.
• Four miles north-east of Haverfordwest, on the B4329 towards Cardigan.
Phone: 01437 731328
www.pembrokeshire.gov.uk

Above left: **Haverfordwest riverside.** The streets around the riverside are home to an array of independent shops and the fortnightly farmers' market.
Above right: **Melin Tregwynt Woollen Mill.** Originally a corn mill on the Tregwynt estate, it was bought by Henry Griffiths for £750 and turned into a weaving mill. Using traditional techniques, the mill creates fashionable designs for customers all over the world.

Milford Haven

The **Cleddau estuary** is a remarkable geographical feature: a ria, or submerged river valley, providing superb shelter for ships. Nelson declared it one of the best natural harbours he had seen anywhere in the world. Once infamous as a hideaway for pirates and smugglers, Milford saw several failed attempts at reinvention – as a naval dockyard, a transatlantic passenger port and (with temporary success) as a fishing harbour. Today, the Milford Haven Waterway is a thriving centre for aquatic sports, with several marinas and sailing schools. It is also one of the UK's main ports for the import of oil.
• The A477 from Pembroke takes you high over the Cleddau estuary. It is worth a detour.

Milford Haven Museum. Housed in a former warehouse on the quayside at Milford Marina, this museum was once a working part of its subject matter. It re-creates Milford Haven's colourful past, focusing, naturally, on the maritime history of the town and the Cleddau waterway.
• The drive down to the harbour reveals the snug shelter provided within its walls.
Phone: 01646 694496

Upton Castle Gardens. These delightful gardens encompass 35 acres of parkland with a wide variety of trees and shrubs on thickly wooded slopes

overlooking the waters of Milford Haven. Particularly noted for its rhododendrons, camellias and magnolias, there are also formal terraces with herbaceous borders, rose gardens and over 250 species of trees and shrubs. There is also a medieval chapel within the grounds.
• Phone: 01646 651782

Pembroke

The attractive main street of Pembroke, with the intimidating mass of the castle at one end, has attractive Georgian architecture, shops and pubs. **Pembroke Dock** is where a largely imported and notoriously unruly workforce constructed 269 wooden-hulled vessels for the Royal Navy between 1814 and 1926. The naval dockyard was overtaken by developments in technology as iron and steel construction became universal. The functional architecture of the buildings has a distinctive charm: there is nothing quite like them anywhere else in Wales.
• Pembroke's castle entrance and main street are a rather steep climb from the quayside car park. www.pembroke-dock.co.uk

Above: **Milford Haven Marina.** This former fishing village saw attempts to develop it as a whaling, naval, passenger and fishing port. Today, the substantial stone walls of the harbour shelter a yacht marina.

Pembroke Dock Gun Tower.
This Martello tower was built to protect the naval dockyard, a vital strategic asset and a likely target for attack. It is equipped as it would have looked when it was in use around the end of the 19th century – complete with cannon and defending soldiers.
• There are quiet corners among the stout buildings where the present day recedes and the past speaks eloquently.
Phone: 01646 622246
www.pembroke-dock.co.uk

Lamphey Bishop's Palace. Near Pembroke, the bishops of St David's built themselves a retreat away from the concerns of church and state. This is where they would enjoy the life of country gentlemen amongst fishponds, orchards, gardens and parkland. The magnificent great hall was built by Henry de Gower, bishop from 1328 to 1347. Later additions include a Tudor chapel which has a very fine east window.
• Some three miles east of Pembroke, on the A4139.
Phone: 01646 672224
www.cadw.wales.gov.uk

St Govan's Chapel and St Justinian's. Sites relating to early Celtic Christianity are very much in evidence throughout Pembrokeshire. On the **Castlemartin peninsula**, St Govan, an Irish hermit, reputedly hid in a crevice in the rock, which miraculously opened for him.

It is on this site that St Govan's Chapel was built. St Justinian's, near St David's, is the site of a medieval chapel and one of the area's many holy wells.
• For St Govan's Chapel, follow the B4319 southward from Pembroke, then take a narrow lane going left after St Petrox.

Preseli Hills

'Bluestone Country'. They are far from being Wales's highest summits, but the Preseli Hills nevertheless hold a powerful attraction. Said to hide the entrance to Annwn, the underworld of Celtic mythology, they are generally accepted to be the place from which the blue stones of Stonehenge were transported.
• From the B4313 and B4329, explore the minor roads over to Newport and Carningli.

Pentre Ifan Burial Chamber.
In prehistoric times, the western extremities of Wales were at the centre of the sea routes linking what we now know as Scotland,

Above left: **St Govan's Chapel.** It is a rather precarious walk down the steep path to St Govans Chapel, but the seclusion and closeness to nature for which its site was chosen make the effort worthwhile.
Above right: **Pembroke Dock waterfront.** Originally a shipbuilding town established in 1814, Pembroke Dock lies on a flat, sheltered area of land on the southern section of the Cleddau River.

Ireland and Brittany. Little wonder, then, that Pembrokeshire has so many cromlechs, standing stones and burial chambers. Pentre Ifan, situated on a gentle hill with wide views towards the sea, surely commemorates someone of great importance during those distant times.

• Signposted from the A487 between Newport and Felindre Farchog.
www.cadw.wales.gov.uk

Gwaun Valley. This tranquil place is a relic of the last Ice Age, when vast amounts of meltwater carved it out as the glaciers retreated. Pontfaen's small church is dedicated to St Brynach, a 6th century missionary who is said to have communed with angels on the summit of **Carningli** in the **Preseli Hills** above the valley. The area has a sense of mystery about it, heightened by the refusal, since the 18th century, of its inhabitants to accept modernisation of the calendar: New Year is celebrated hereabouts each January 13th.

• Follow the narrow road to Pontfaen from the B4313 south-east of Fishguard.

St David's

Saint David, the patron saint of Wales, was born around 462 AD on the site of the chapel named after his mother, St Non, near the little city that now bears his name. Following a lifetime of

dedication to God, he came to be revered as a great Christian leader. The magnificent cathedral of St David's, built from the 12th century onwards, graces the secluded valley of the River Alun, where, despite being hidden from the sea, earlier churches were destroyed by Vikings. In contrast with the ascetic lifestyle of the Celtic saints, the medieval bishops of St David's enjoyed great wealth – the extravagant architecture of the Bishop's Palace reflects the status of Henry de Gower and his successors as major figures of church and state.

• Reach this westernmost part of Wales via the M4, A48, A40 and A487 – or by rail to Fishguard or Haverfordwest.
www.stdavids.co.uk

Porthclais, Abereiddi, Porthgain, Abercastle. With no railway within reach, the small ports of this far western coast were vital for the export of local slate, granite, and gravel for building and road making, and for the import of goods to sustain these remote communities. The last cargo of stone was shipped out from Porthgain in 1929, but the tiny harbour, with its rusting cranes, bollards and machinery, remains full of character.

Above: **St David's Cathedral.**
Marvellously impressive when seen from the paths that lead down from the square above, the cathedral and the adjacent Bishop's Palace constitute the most important religious site in Wales.

• Between St David's and Fishguard, on minor roads that reward patience.

Solva

Of the small ports around **St Bride's Bay**, Solva grew to be the most important for fishing and for trade with Ireland, Bristol and elsewhere. Its zigzag entrance and narrow proportions provided excellent shelter and made it easy to defend against the Vikings. There was some small-scale shipbuilding here during the 19th century and there are the remains of several lime kilns at the harbour. Nowadays, it is a popular cruising destination for yacht owners, for whom negotiating the entrance – past the memorably named **St Elvis Rocks** – is a satisfying navigational exercise.

• Carefully negotiate the narrow roads down to the harbour from the A487 east of St David's. www.solva.net

Middle Mill Woollen Mill, Solva. This mill has been in continuous production since it opened in 1907. Dyed and spun yarn is mainly woven into floor rugs and carpets. The original waterwheel is undergoing restoration, and the machinery is now powered by electricity. The factory contains five Dobcross looms and their associated warping and wefting machinery.

• Just inland from Solva, along narrow lanes.

Phone: 01437 721112
www.solvawoollenmill.co.uk

....

Tenby

Picturesque Tenby has been one
of the main tourism centres of
Wales since the arrival of the
railway in 1863, but the attractive
town and cosy harbour, centred
between two fabulous sandy
beaches, were popular
destinations for artists and
travellers long before then.
Tenby's origins are as a working
port, one of the most important
in Wales during the Middle Ages.
The Norman presence, centred
on the castle, generated trade
with France, Spain and Portugal.
Many buildings reflect the port's
continuing prosperity during

Tudor times as a centre for
fishing and coal export.
The Victorians realised, though,
that it was in their interest to
develop the town as a resort,
and leisure boating, bathing and
promenading gradually took over
from commercial craft.
• Alive with holiday fun in
summer, Tenby has all the
resources of a popular resort,
including excellent eating places.
www.visitpembrokeshire.com

Above: Tenby Harbour.
The scenic location and colourful
buildings of Tenby's picturesque
harbour, used by fishing boats and
pleasure craft, have long attracted
artists and holidaymakers.

Tenby Museum and Art Gallery.
Founded in 1878, this is one of
the oldest independent museums
in Wales; it is run largely by an
enthusiastic band of volunteers.
The displays cover archaeology,
geology, natural history and the
maritime and social history of
Tenby and south Pembrokeshire
from the Stone Age to the present
day. The **Wilfred Harrison Gallery**
houses a collection of works by
Augustus John, Gwen John,
Nina Hamnet, EJ Head and
other local artists.
Phone: 01834 842809
www.tenbymuseum.org.uk

Tenby Tudor Merchant's House.
This late-15th century house
is a fine example of a wealthy
merchant's home, reflecting
family life in Tudor times, when
Tenby was a thriving port.
The Flemish-style round chimney
at the back is evidence of the
presence of people from the
Low Countries in southern
Pembrokeshire at the time.
The family would have lived
on the first and second floors,
with servants preparing food
on the ground floor.
• On Quay Hill, off Tudor Square,
close to the railway station and
less than a mile (about 1.5km)
from the Pembrokeshire
Coast Path.
Phone: 01834 842279
www.nationaltrust.org.uk

Festivals and events

Newport Bay Spring Festival.
This four-day sports, cultural
and entertainment festival is
held at Newport in northern
Pembrokeshire over the early-
May holiday. It features music,
dance, arts and crafts exhibitions,
cycling, walking, running, a mini
regatta and horse riding events.
• Newport is on the A487
between Fishguard and Cardigan.
Phone: 01239 820912
www.newport-pembs.co.uk

Fishguard Folk Festival. Held at
the end of **May**, this is a weekend
of folk music, song and dance.
Ever-increasing in popularity,
it is being noticed more and more
on a national stage. There are
concerts, dance displays, meet
the artist events, instrumental
and voice workshops, informal
music and song sessions, and
a real ale bar.
• Venues include the Royal Oak
pub and Theatr Gwaun, both of

Above left: **Tudor Merchant's House.**
The Flemish influences on the
Tudor Merchant's House in Tenby
are evidence of how the long
coastline of Wales has, for many
centuries, opened the way for
contact and trade with other
countries.
Above right: **Fishguard Harbour.**
From modest origins as a fishing
port, Fishguard grew into a
significant shipbuilding centre and
an important passenger port for
Ireland – the infamous pirate
Bartholomew Roberts (Black Bart)
was born near here.

which have programmes and information.
Phone: 01348 875183
www.pembrokeshire-folk-music.co.uk

St David's Cathedral Festival.
For nine days annually, in late **May** and early **June**, St David's Cathedral is host to a feast of classical music. The reverberant acoustics and inspiring architecture of the nave, including its 16th century Irish oak ceiling, provide a concert venue of rare atmosphere. Under the musical direction of cathedral organist Timothy Noon, the St David's Cathedral Choir and the Festival Orchestra combine their abilities with singers and instrumentalists representing a range of styles

and eras.
• There are steep paths down from the square and more level access from the signed main entrance to the cathedral.
Phone: 01437 721682
www.stdavidscathedral.org.uk

Pembrokeshire Fish Week.
Late **June** sees a programme of more than 50 family-friendly events and activities around Pembrokeshire. In this food-lover's paradise, there are opportunities to try speciality fish and shellfish dishes, and to attend wine tastings and cookery demonstrations. There are also competitions for anglers – coarse, fly and sea – along with have-a-go sessions for newcomers.

• Upwards of 160 restaurants, food shops and pubs are involved in the food events; demonstrations by celebrity chefs are at the Torch Theatre, Milford Haven; angling is at Milford Haven (sea), Llawhaden Reservoir (coarse) and other inland waters. Phone: 01437 776168 www.pembrokeshire.gov.uk/fishweek

Haverfordwest Festival Week. Held in early **July**, the week includes spectacular re-enactments by the Knights of the Longshanks – who, from their base at Haverfordwest Castle, sally forth into the town, taking hostage any unfortunate civic dignitary who crosses their path. Medieval battle re-enactments also take place at the castle and you may visit the medieval fayre, where a range of produce is sold, and see how the knights lived. There are also Victorian-themed events and the week ends with the Haverfordwest Carnival.
• Phone: 01437 763427 www.haverfordwest-wales.info

Pembrokeshire Agricultural Show. In mid **August**, the Withybush Showground near Haverfordwest welcomes some 100,000 visitors to one of the

Above: **Pembrokeshire Fish Week.** Seafood tapas tastings, rock pool rambles, snorkel safari and children's angling open days are just some of the activities at this festival.

largest regional agricultural shows in Wales. The three days of countryside activity and fun enthral local residents and visiting city dwellers alike. Animals ranging from cattle, sheep and horses to poultry, dogs and cage birds compete for honours. Vintage tractors, the Welsh Axe Team, sheepdog trials and show jumping add to the entertainment.

• Withybush is just north of Haverfordwest, on the A40. Phone: 01437 764331 www.pembrokeshirecountyshow. co.uk

The Really Wild Food and Countryside Festival.
With the botanist Professor David Bellamy as its patron, The Really Wild Food and Countryside Festival is a celebration of foods and countryside crafts that originate from the wild. Exhibition stands and demonstrations show how we can all explore, understand and make use of wild materials and ingredients in the same way that our ancestors did, but with some new ideas.

• Held at St David's Football Ground in early **September**. Phone: 01348 891381 www.reallywildfestival.co.uk

Tenby Arts Festival.
In combination with the attractiveness and historical interest of the town itself, this festival's programme of instrumental music, choral performances, talks, drama, art

exhibitions, films, workshops and beach activities will ensure that a late-season break in Tenby will be enjoyable and memorable.
• Many of Tenby's churches, museums, galleries, restaurants, pubs and halls echo to the sounds of the festival's performances, and the applause of appreciative audiences, during late **September**.
Phone: 01834 845341
www.tenbyartsfest.co.uk

Tenby Blues Festival.
This new annual event provides a platform for Blues artists – of international, national and local stature. Audiences get to see, hear, meet and talk to some of the top bluesmen in the world, and to hear home-grown talent.

Events large and small are held at some of Tenby's numerous bars and clubs, with all main concerts taking place at the De Valence Pavilion on Upper Frog Street.
• Held at the end of **November**, when Tenby is relatively quiet – exploring the streets, restaurants and pubs of the little town, as the nights draw in, is a joy.
www.tenbyblues.co.uk

Above left: **Really Wild Food.** This two day event celebrates food and craft from the wild and includes walks, talks, chef demonstrations and food and craft producers.
Above right: **Tenby Blues Festival.** Held in a beautiful seaside town, the Tenby Blues Festival has a fantastic programme of performances, workshops, talks and films.

Carmarthenshire

Carmarthen, Carreg Cennen Castle, Dinefwr Park,
Laugharne, Dolaucothi Gold Mines, the National
Botanic Garden of Wales, Aberglasney, the National
Wool Museum and the National Coracle Centre.

Carmarthenshire towns.
The main towns of the county vary enormously in character. Industrial **Llanelli**, in the south, was a prominent centre of tinplate production, an activity that continues there today. The **Millennium Coastal Park** has reclaimed many industrial sites for public enjoyment. **Burry Port** was built for the export of coal from the Gwendraeth valley, to which it was linked by rail.
Ammanford grew as the main town of the western, anthracite-producing region of the great coalfield of southern Wales.
Llandeilo and **Newcastle Emlyn**, in complete contrast, are historic market towns serving, respectively, the Tywi and Teifi valleys.

• The A-roads will get you around, but be sure to seek out minor routes.
www.carmartheshire.gov.uk

....

Carmarthen

To the Romans, Carmarthen was Moridunum, the Sea Fort, a secure place to import the supplies that sustained their presence in the region. The same imperative drove the Normans to build their castle overlooking the river. The town's Welsh name

Above: **National Botanic Garden.**
The spectacular Great Glasshouse, designed by Foster & Partners, at the National Botanic Garden provides a favourable environment for tropical and desert plants.

– **Caerfyrddin** – derives from Myrddin Emrys, Merlin the Magician, who is said to have been born here. During the Middle Ages, Carmarthen became one of the main market towns of Wales, its huddle of narrow streets crowded around the castle. It remains the regional administrative and shopping centre today. The imposing **County Hall**, in the style of a French chateau, dominates the view of the town from the river.

• Some fifteen miles from the western end of the M4 motorway, along the A48 dual carriageway. www.carmarthenshire.gov.uk

Roman and Merlin connections. Archaeological evidence of early settlement around Carmarthen includes the Iron Age hill fort at **Merlin's Hill**, Abergwili. Nature trails take you to the hilltop site where you may imagine Merlin enjoying the same views.
In Carmarthen itself, the Roman amphitheatre was just one of the structures, along with forum, temple and baths, that were essential in a provincial town of substance.
Phone: 01267 237808
www.merlinshill.com

Oriel Myrddin Gallery. With its exhibits approved for quality by the Crafts Council, this regional gallery and crafts centre is well worth a visit. Open all year, it puts on an ever-changing programme of exhibitions, creative workshops

and activities for all ages.
• Located in a listed Victorian art school in Church Lane, on the eastern side of the town, opposite St Peter's Church.
Phone: 01267 222775
www.carmarthenshire.gov.uk

Carmarthenshire County Museum.

The county's past is chronicled at this informative museum. The building was once the palace of the bishops of St David's, and it was here that the New Testament was first translated into Welsh in 1567. The displays feature prehistoric remains, Roman artefacts, landscape paintings, costume, decorative items, Welsh furniture and much more. Don't miss the Victorian schoolroom and the carefully preserved remains of the ancient Carmarthen oak: Merlin the Magician was said to have prophesied that if this tree fell, so would the town.
• Set in delightful parkland at Abergwili, just off the A40 towards Llandeilo.
Phone: 01267 228696
www.carmarthenshire.gov.uk

Above left: **Dinefwr Castle.** The prominent fortress of Dinefwr is one of several castles that punctuate the green and gentle landscape of the Tywi Valley (page 43).
Above right: **Carmarthenshire County Museum.** The County Museum presents many aspects of Carmarthenshire's rich and varied past from local archaeology to the homefront in World War II.

Gwili Railway. This trip down memory lane starts at **Bronwydd Arms**, north of Carmarthen, and follows a section of the old Great Western line that once ran to Aberystwyth. For much of its route, the steam train runs alongside the **River Gwili**, passing through a pleasant farming landscape. At its terminus, **Llwyfan Cerrig**, where stone was once loaded from the quarry that forms an impressive backdrop, there is a restored station building from **Felinfach**. You might also enjoy a ride on the miniature railway.

• Bronwydd Arms is some three miles north of Carmarthen, on the A484.
Phone: 01267 230666
www.gwili-railway.co.uk

Kidwelly

As early as 1223, there is a record of Henry III licensing one Robert de Cadwely, Magister Navis – ship's master – to trade wool and animal skins to France, and to bring back wine and olive oil. The 13th century castle and its great gatehouse, completed in 1422, are remarkably well preserved. Kidwelly gives an unusually complete insight into the evolution of a medieval fortress into an increasingly domesticated, though still very grand, household. By the 19th century, when coal mining boomed in the **Gwendraeth valley** inland, ships had grown to a size that the silt-prone estuary could

not handle and the town has retained its compact charm.
• Ten miles south of Carmarthen, on the A484.
www.kidwelly.gov.uk

Kidwelly Industrial Museum.
Wales once produced much of the world's tinplate, which was used for the tin cans that were such a leap forward in food storage during the 19th century. Llanelli grew to be the largest centre of production but there was also a tinplate works, set in attractive countryside, at Kidwelly. It is now home to a fascinating museum, which also describes other industries including coal mining and brick making that evolved in this largely rural county.
• From the A484 Kidwelly bypass, follow signs for Mynydd-y-Garreg.
Phone: 01554 891078
www.carmarthenshire.gov.uk

Laugharne

Dylan Thomas and his wife Caitlin first moved here in 1938, a year after getting married, and returned to settle at **The**

Above left: **Gwili Railway.** The Gwili Railway is a living reminder of a Great Western Railway branch line set in the breathtaking Carmarthenshire Hills.
Above right: **Kidwelly Castle.** Kidwelly Castle stands on a steep bluff overlooking the River Gwendraeth. It is remarkably well preserved, the most arresting feature being the Great Gatehouse.

Boathouse in 1948. The **Dylan Thomas Trail** will lead you to many sites associated with Wales's greatest English-language poet – in Carmarthenshire, Swansea, Pembrokeshire and Ceredigion. His presence still pervades Laugharne. He would work intensively in his writing shed above The Boathouse (now a museum to his life and work) before adjourning to his favoured drinking haunt, **Brown's Hotel**, in the village. Dylan and Caitlin are buried in **St Martin's churchyard**, their grave marked by a simple white cross. Inside the church is a replica of the memorial stone to him in Poet's Corner, Westminster Abbey.

• Laugharne is on the A4066, four miles south of St Clears. Walk along roads and paths familiar to Dylan Thomas. www.laugharne.co.uk

Llansteffan Castle. Sunset is a great time to visit **Ferryside**, on the eastern shore of the **Towy estuary**, to savour the romantic sight of the ruins of **Llansteffan Castle** high on the cliff-top opposite. Established in the early 12th century, on the site of an Iron Age promontory fort, it was held by the de Camville family of Norman barons for much of the Middle Ages.

• Follow minor roads west from Kidwelly, with great views of the Gwendraeth estuary. www.cadw.wales.gov.uk

West Wales Centre for the Crafts. Located at **St Clears**, this multi-role centre has a large gallery featuring work by local artists, several of whom work in the associated studios and workshops. It also has a coffee-house restaurant. Check out the events programme for talks and tuition in a range of creative activities.

• St Clears is nine miles west of Carmarthen, on the A40 dual carriageway. www.artswales.org

Llandeilo

Llandeilo is a small, but thriving, market town in Carmarthenshire, situated on the edge of the Brecon Beacons National Park. Llandeilo is named after one of the most eminent and celebrated Celtic saints of the 6th century, Saint Teilo, who established a small monastic settlement on the site of the present day church. Its narrow streets and historic buildings make this an attractive town. The bridge over the River Towy was built in 1848 and is the largest single span stone bridge in Wales.

Dinefwr Park and Newton House. Just west of Llandeilo, this medieval deer park, delightfully

Left: **The Boathouse at Laugharne. It is little wonder that Dylan Thomas was inspired to such flights of genius in his descriptions of sea and coastline. This is where he lived and worked.**

landscaped and extended in 1775 by **Lancelot "Capability" Brown**, is home to around a hundred fallow deer and a small herd of an ancient breed of long-horned white cattle. Walks lead to **Dinefwr Castle**, stronghold of the Lord Rhys, from which there are wide views of the gentle **Tywi valley**. Newton House, built in 1660 but now with a Victorian Gothic Revival façade and fountain garden, contains an exhibition about its history and a tea room with views of the deer park.

• A short drive or a moderate walk from the centre of Llandeilo. Phone: 01558 824512 www.nationaltrust.org.uk

Aberglasney. The 15th century bard Lewis Glyn Cothi wrote of a white-painted house here, surrounded by nine gardens, orchards, vineyards and large oak trees. It was one of the earliest descriptions of any house and garden in Wales. In the subsequent ownership of the Bishop of St David's and a series of wealthy families, the estate was enlarged and improved, but its fortunes eventually declined and it became derelict.

Since 1995, the Aberglasney Restoration Trust has worked hard to reverse this sorry fate and "The Garden Lost in Time" is once again amongst Wales's finest gardens. The intriguing yew tunnel, believed to be over a thousand years old, and many 16th and 17th century features have survived.

• Off the A40 west of Llandeilo and close to the National Botanic Garden.
Phone: 01558 668998
www.aberglasney.org

Iron-Age fort at Garn Goch, near Bethlehem. One of the largest Iron Age hill forts in Wales stands 700 feet (213m) above sea level in the Brecon Beacons National Park. Its extensive ramparts follow the contours of the hill. The ravages of the past two thousand years have reduced them to lines of rubble but they once stood tall and would have been a daunting sight. Bethlehem – named, as are many Welsh villages, after its chapel – sees many visitors in the weeks before Christmas, when its seasonal post office opens for the franking of cards and the sale of commemorative covers.
• Signposted along a minor road heading north-eastwards from Llandeilo.

Carreg Cennen Castle.
Few castles anywhere command a location as spectacular or as difficult to attack as this. On its precipitous 320 foot (100m) limestone crag, in the far west of the Brecon Beacons

Above: **Aberglasney.**
Small but perfectly formed, the gardens of Aberglasney are within easy reach of the National Botanic Garden. These remarkable attractions provide two excellent reasons to visit Carmarthenshire.

National Park, this atmospheric stronghold is evocative of legend or fairy tale. Its origins are obscure but it fell alternately into Welsh and English hands during the Middle Ages, before being largely dismantled in 1462. A visit is made all the more memorable if you descend the dark and narrow passageway leading to a small natural cave beneath the fortifications, which was possibly inhabited during prehistoric times. It would have been an uncomfortable hideaway for non-combatants as battle raged above.

• Follow signs to Trapp and the castle from the A483 south of Llandeilo.
Phone: 01558 822291
www.cadw.wales.gov.uk

Dryslwyn Castle and Paxton's Tower. Recent excavation has uncovered much evidence concerning this hilltop defensive site. Originally a castle of the native Welsh princes of Deheubarth, it was taken by the forces of Edward I in 1287, but returned to Welsh hands – those of Owain Glyndŵr – in 1403. Nearby Paxton's Tower was built in 1811 as a monument to Lord Nelson and provides a tremendous elevated viewpoint.

• Five miles west of Llandeilo along the A40/B4300.
www.cadw.wales.gov.uk
www.nationaltrust.org.uk

National Botanic Garden of Wales. This is a national treasure for the whole of the UK. It is a botanic garden in the full sense, being a centre for research as well as a gloriously attractive place to enjoy flowers, plants and trees. Built on the once-neglected Middleton estate, where the fine house burned down in 1931, the gardens include the sheltered double-walled garden, original water features, many new plantings and the Wallace Garden, honouring the famous Welsh botanist Alfred Russell Wallace. The National Botanic Garden also boasts the world's largest single span glasshouse and one of Europe's longest herbaceous borders, all set within a partially restored Regency Park.

• Easily reached via its own junction on the A48, close to the western end of the M4.
Phone: 01558 668768
www.gardenofwales.org.uk

Talley Abbey. This was the only abbey in Wales to be founded by the Premonstratensians, or White Canons, whose way of life combined Cistercian and Augustinian principles.

Right: **National Botanic Garden of Wales.** Working with the National Museum Wales and the Countryside Council for Wales, the National Botanic Garden is conserving some of Wales's rarest flowers and trees, and the Great Glasshouse is a refuge for some of the world's most endangered plants.

It was founded for them by their supporter Lord Rhys ap Gruffudd late in the 12th century, but it was poorly funded and never became a leading religious house.
• Idyllically situated on the B4302 north of Llandeilo. www.cadw.wales.gov.uk

Llandovery

Park beneath the castle and admire the remarkable stainless steel sculpture of **Llywelyn ap Gruffydd Fychan**, loyal supporter of Owain Glyndŵr, then call at the Heritage Centre, with its statue of a cattle drover outside. Along the street is the **memorial church to William Williams of Pantycelyn**. He was a poet, a preacher and the best-loved of Welsh hymn writers. Of more than nine hundred hymns penned by him, 'Guide Me O Thou Great Redeemer' is perhaps the most familiar and inspiring, whether it is sung in competent four-part harmony by a Welsh congregation or roared by tens of thousands of rugby supporters in the emotional cauldron of Cardiff's Millennium Stadium.
• From the M4, follow the A483 and A40 to the inland part of Carmarthenshire.

Dolaucothi Gold Mines.
The appeal of western Wales to the Romans derived largely from the minerals they extracted here which included a substantial quantity of gold, likely to have

been transported under heavy guard to the empire's mints in Lyon and Rome. They left some two kilometres of underground workings at Dolaucothi, near Pumsaint, a site that was mined again in the 19th and 20th centuries, and continues occasionally to be explored for possibilities. Guided tours take you through Roman and more recent tunnels, and you may experience the frustrations of prospectors as you attempt to pan for gold.

• Off the A482 mid-way between Llandovery and Lampeter.
Phone: 01558 650177
www.nationaltrust.org.uk

Llanelli

Historically a minor town on the mouth of the River Loughor, Llanelli grew significantly in the 18th and 19th centuries with the mining of coal and later the tinplate industry. It became such a significant regional producer of tin that it was referred to as "Tinopolis" by the latter half of the 19th century. The closure of coal mines and competition from overseas steel plants meant that Llanelli, like many other towns in

Above: **Dolaucothi Gold Mines.** Located in the picturesque Cothi Valley this site of industry dates back almost 2000 years. Stout footwear is essential for the underground tour.

south Wales saw significant and sustained economic decline from the late 1970s. Today, Llanelli is an attractive town with a proud rugby tradition.

Llanelli Millennium Coastal Park. Occupying 20 kilometres of coastline along the Burry Estuary, Llanelli's Millennium Coastal Park looks across to the scenic Gower Peninsula. It features a range of leisure attractions and natural habitats, linked by a coastal path and cycleway extending from The National Wetlands Centre Wales, at Penclacwydd, to Pembrey Country Park.

Parc Howard Museum and Art Gallery, Llanelli. Explore Llanelli's past at this gallery set in a fine house built for the Buckley family of brewers in 1885. The surrounding parkland and gardens were donated to the town by the Howard family in 1912. Exhibits include a collection of Llanelli pottery, local paintings and many items related to the history of the town.
• North of Llanelli, off the A476 towards Cross Hands.
Phone: 01554 772029

Theatr Elli, Llanelli, and The Lyric, Carmarthen. Regional theatre is alive and well in Wales, with venues such as these putting on lively progammes of theatre, music, comedy, films and other

entertainment in both English and Welsh.
• Programmes in local newspapers and from Tourist Information Centres.
Phone: 0845 226 3509 (Lyric)
Phone: 0845 226 3508 (Elli)
www.carmarthenshiretheatres.co.uk

Newcastle Emlyn

National Coracle Centre, Cenarth. Here, the river Teifi tumbles over the impressive **Cenarth Falls**, one of Wales's first tourist attractions, much visited by Victorian travellers. The National Coracle Centre, which is housed in a 17th century flour mill that is driven by a water wheel, has an international collection of coracles from as far afield as America, India, Vietnam, Tibet and Iraq. The local version evolved as a lightweight one-man craft suited to netting salmon and trout on the rapid waters of the Teifi.
• Three miles west of Newcastle Emlyn, on the A484 towards Cardigan.
Phone: 01239 710980
www.coracle-centre.co.uk

Above left: **Parc Howard Museum and Art Gallery, Llanelli.** Occupying a fine house set in attractive gardens.
Above right: **National Coracle Centre.** The skills involved in making the basket-like frame of a coracle – which is then covered in tarred canvas – are displayed at the National Coracle Centre.

National Wool Museum, Drefach Felindre. At the restored Cambrian Mills near Newcastle Emlyn, discover the fascinating history of the Welsh woollen industry, which was a vital contributor to the economy in many parts of Wales. Experience the clatter of the complicated machinery, hear the stories of the mill workers, and see the cloth in all its richly coloured and patterned glory. This fine museum, part of the National Museum Wales, also features items from the national textile collection. There is something for everyone to enjoy: you can even try your hand at carding, spinning and sewing.
• Some twelve miles north of Carmarthen, on the A484.
www.museumwales.ac.uk

Pendine

Pendine Museum of Speed.
Overlooking one of the longest and smoothest stretches of sand in the UK, the museum tells the story of the land speed record attempts and racing that went on there. The main exhibit is "Babs", the car used by Parry Thomas for his fatal attempt at the record in 1927. The car was buried in the sands for many years before being recovered and restored by enthusiasts.

Left and above: **National Wool Museum.** Every aspect of the production of wool in its varied forms is explained at this museum.

• Continue along the A4066 from Laugharne until you reach the wide sands of Pendine.
Phone: 01994 453488
www.carmarthenshire.gov.uk

....

Hywel Dda Gardens and Interpretive Centre, Whitland.

Hywel ap Cadell ruled much of Wales during the ninth and early tenth centuries. He devised a remarkably wise and humane legal system, which remained in force until Henry VIII's Act of Union with England in 1536. Hywel's emphasis on compensating the victim rather than punishing the offender, and his enlightened views on the rights of women earned him the name Hywel Dda, Howell the Good. This attractive garden in his memory is said to be the only one in Europe dedicated to the law.
• Five miles west of St Clear's on the A448 towards Haverfordwest.
Phone: 01994 240867
www.hywel-dda.co.uk

....

Festivals and events

United Counties Show.

This two-day agricultural show, held each **August**, has drawn the crowds for more than a century. It promotes agriculture in west Wales through impressive livestock competitions in the main ring, a wide variety of stands and stalls, a craft marquee and a large food hall.
• Phone: 01267 232141
www.unitedcounties.co.uk

Welsh Game Fair.

Held in **June**, the Welsh Game Fair is an atmospheric gathering for country folk and all who enjoy the traditions of rural life, including working-dog enthusiasts and participants in shooting, fishing and equestrian pursuits. Held in the pleasant surroundings of Gelli Aur Country Park, the fair has a lively programme of events and a range of food and craft stalls.
• Phone: 01267 281410

Merlin, Magic and Mystery Festival.

Carmarthen steps back into its medieval past each **June**, with an array of entertainment including street performers, magicians, storytellers and medieval re-enactments. There is also a local arts and crafts market, live music and a parade. The festival brings to life the town's legendary connection with the Arthurian magician Merlin.
• Phone: 01554 747542
www.carmarthenshire.gov.uk

Left: **Merlin Magic and Mystery Festival.** This Arthurian festival brings a touch of magic to Carmarthen with medieval re-enactors, stuntmen, jesters and magicians.

Swansea and Gower

The bustling city, the Swansea Valley and nearby
Gower feature the Swansea Maritime Quarter,
Margam Abbey, National Waterfront Museum,
Glynn Vivian Gallery, Dylan Thomas Centre, Swansea
Festival of Music and the Arts, Swansea Grand
Theatre, and Brangwyn Hall.

Cynonville

South Wales Miners' Museum.
Located within the Afan Argoed
Countryside Centre, this small
but moving museum depicts the
story of the miner and his family
as they coped with the dangers
of the job in the great coalfield of
the south Wales Valleys. A range
of outdoor exhibits includes a
blacksmith's workshop.
• Exit J40 of the M4 to the A4107
and follow signs to Cymmer and
Argoed Forest Park.
Phone: 01639 850564
www.npt.gov.uk

Gower

The Gower Peninsula. In 1956,
Gower became the first place in
Britain to be designated an Area
of Outstanding Natural Beauty.
Within its compact dimensions
you will find spectacular cliffs,
magnificent beaches, elevated
heathland, lush meadows, oak
woods, salt marshes and sand
dunes. Rich evidence of human
habitation – including Neolithic
and Bronze Age sites, medieval

Above: **Three Cliffs Bay.**
Getting to this marvellous place
involves a moderate walk through
sand dunes, from Southgate, but
means that when you get there you
will find no cars or buildings to
spoil the view.

castles, ancient hedgerows and farm boundaries, and 18th century parkland – underlines its appeal through the centuries. Former fishing villages, including Mumbles and Port Eynon, have become popular holiday and leisure destinations.
• Head westward from Swansea on the A4118 – or follow the walking and cycling route around Swansea Bay to Mumbles.

Gower Heritage Centre, Parkmill. The whole family can learn all about the rural life of Gower at this entertaining attraction. Parkmill is a water-powered cornmill and sawmill where you will find farm animals, mini-tractor rides and a puppet theatre.

• On the A4118, a couple of miles past Swansea airport.
Phone: 01792 371206
www.gowerheritagecentre.co.uk

The Castles of Gower. Oystermouth is the finest of Gower's castles. It was founded by William de Londres early in the 12th century and became the main residence of the de Braose family, Lords of Gower. **Loughor Castle** has a 13th century tower on top of a 12th century earthwork, built on the corner of a Roman fort. **Weobley Castle** is a picturesque medieval fortified manor house with substantial remains dating from the early 14th century. **Oxwich Castle** consists of the remains of a sumptuous, mock-fortified

manor built by the Mansel family during the 16th century.

• Follow the A4067 to Mumbles for Oystermouth. The A4118 takes you into Gower from Swansea. www.cadw.wales.gov.uk

Margam

Margam Abbey. Set in 1000 acres of glorious parkland, Margam Country Park offers a variety of wildlife as well as a magnificent 18th century Orangery, monastic gardens and an impressive Tudor-Gothic style Victorian Mansion House which was built between 1830 and 1840. In its beautiful parkland surroundings, Margam Abbey Church (founded in 1147) is the only Cistercian foundation in Wales where the nave is intact and still used for Christian worship. Other remains of the original monastery include a twelve-sided chapter house in early-English style. The excellent **Margam Abbey Stones Museum** holds a small but very significant collection of inscribed Celtic and Roman stones and crosses, some of which were found within the local area, and includes the great **Wheel Cross of Conbelin**.

Above left: **Weobley Castle.** Better described as a fortified manor house than a fortress, Weobley Castle was built as an elegant residence for the de la Bere family.
Above right: **Margam Country Park.** A great place to enjoy scenic beauty, history and wildlife.

• Close to J38 on the M4 motorway. Phone: 01639 881635 www.neath-porttalbot.gov.uk/margampark

Mumbles

Mumbles is one the UK's most attractive coastal towns. As early as 1806, a railway was built between Oystermouth and Swansea. Initially this was to carry coal in horse-drawn trucks, but the novel idea of transporting people was soon seized upon and the first passenger railway service in the world began here in March 1807. Steam trains were later introduced and Mumbles became a popular day out. The line was extended and in 1898 the pier was constructed to serve as its new terminus. Mumbles has a good showing of craft shops.

• The A4067 and the bayside walking and cycle route are pleasing approaches. www.visitswanseabay.com

Arthur's Stone. The capstone of this neolithic tomb on the summit of **Cefn-y-Bryn** weighs over twenty-five tons but legend has it that it was a pebble from King Arthur's shoe, thrown across the Burry Estuary. The stone is also said to make the journey to **Three Cliffs Bay** every New Year's Eve to drink from the sea.

• Seek out a local map showing paths to Cefn-y-bryn from Nicholaston on the A4118.

Peter Gill And Associates

Radnor Court

256 Cowbridge Road East

CARDIFF

CF5 1YW

Graffeg Publishing thanks you for purchasing this book. If you'd like to be kept up to date with future titles please complete the card and return to us.

☐ Please keep me up to date with future titles

Title/Mr/Mrs/Ms

Name

Address

City

Post code

Email

I am interested in books about Wales and the following subjects

☐ Heritage   ☐ Seascapes
☐ Food   ☐ Festivals
☐ Castles   ☐ Attractions
☐ Villages   ☐ Arts
☐ Cottages   ☐ Music
☐ Houses   ☐ Guides
☐ Gardens   ☐ Hotels

GRAFFEG™

www.graffeg.com
+44(0)29 2037 7312

Neath

Neath Abbey. Originally founded as a daughter house of Savigny in 1130, Neath Abbey was absorbed into the Cistercian order in 1147 and was described as the 'Fairest Abbey in all Wales' by the Tudor historian John Leland. The site has enjoyed varying fortunes, even serving as an early copper works after dissolution. Situated near an industrial area, the abbey's location on the banks of the **Tennant Canal** makes it a tranquil place to visit.

• From J43 on the M4, follow signs for Skewen and the Abbey. www.cadw.wales.gov.uk

Neath Canal. This scenic example of one of the main means of transport during the Industrial Revolution was made famous by the novelist Alexander Cordell in 'Song of the Earth.' Today, passenger craft navigate the restored section of the canal north of Resolven. The **'Enfys'**, a purpose-built boat for the disabled, is available for charter and the **'Thomas Dadford'**, a twelve-seater trip boat, operates from Neath. The canal's towpath provides a great walk to Aberdulais, where the basin has a skew bridge and a twelve-arch aqueduct over the River Neath.

Above: **Resolven, Neath Canal.** The towpaths of the Neath Canal lead past fascinating sites of industrial heritage, now restored to green again.

• Aberdulais and Resolven are north-east of Neath, on the A465.
www.waterscape.com

Neath Museum and Art Gallery.
Situated in the town centre, this museum's two galleries cover the archaeology and natural history of the Neath area. Call in to meet Sebastian, the Roman soldier, who will tell you how tough life was in Neath's Roman fort, or try your hand at grinding corn.
• Approach from J41 or J44.
Phone: 01639 645726
www.npt.gov.uk/museums

Pontardawe Arts Centre.
Pontardawe Arts Centre has gained a reputation as a fine cultural venue. The theatre hosts professional work of the highest calibre, from classical music to drama and dance, literature and children's theatre to blues and world music: something for everyone to enjoy. Regular cinema showings provide the opportunity to enjoy the latest blockbusters as well as the less mainstream art-house movies provided by the local film society.
Oriel Lliw Gallery is the place to while away the time at the regular exhibitions. **Pontardawe Folk Festival**, an annual celebration of world music and dance with, as you might expect, a strong Celtic representation, is held in the town each August.
• Follow the A4067 from J45 on the M4. Phone: 01792 863722
www.npt.gov.uk/pontardawearts centre

Cefn Coed Colliery Museum.
Wonder at the harsh life of the collier underground as you view the magnificent steam winding engine, the simulated coal-mine gallery and the displays of mining tools and equipment at this museum housed in the original buildings of the former Cefn Coed Colliery. Miner's lamps and other souvenirs are sold at the gift shop.
• At Crynant, north of Neath on the A4109.
Phone: 01639 750556
www.npt.gov.uk/museums

Swansea

Swansea's Maritime Quarter.
Former docklands have been redeveloped to give Swansea one of the most attractive waterfronts you will find anywhere, all within a few minutes' walk of the city centre. The grand headquarters of the Swansea Harbour Trust, built in 1902, is now the five-star Morgan's boutique hotel, a comfortable stopover favoured by stars of stage, screen and sport, and a great place for a snack or a meal in the fine restaurant.
The Pumphouse, which once housed the steam engines that provided hydraulic power for the swing bridge, dock gates, cranes

Left: **Neath Abbey.** Graceful Gothic arches hint at the past splendour of Neath Abbey, a place of tangible sanctity in a region of earthly endeavour and industry.

and dockside machinery nearby is a pub and restaurant. The impressive **National Waterfront Museum** is the place to learn all about the industrial, maritime and social history of the whole of Wales.
• Between the shopping area and the beach. Underpasses and footbridges will get you past the busy seafront road.

Glynn Vivian Gallery. Make your way here to view a broad spectrum of visual art including works by old masters and by modern painters and sculptors. There is an internationally renowned collection of porcelain and Swansea pottery.
• On Alexandra Road.

Phone: 01792 516900
www.swansea.gov.uk

Egypt Centre. University of Wales Swansea, is one of the most popular centres in the UK for the study of Egyptology, and this centre, which is open to the public, gives an authoritative introduction to the dynasties that once ruled along the Nile.
• The university occupies a large campus at Singleton Park, west of the city centre.
Phone: 01790 295960
www.swan.ac.uk/egypt

National Waterfront Museum. The story of Wales at work in industries old and new is brought to life by fascinating exhibits and informative multimedia

presentations at this superb new museum in Swansea's Maritime Quarter. A tremendous selection of items is on display, from wonderful paintings and intricate ship models to large vehicles and powerful machinery; from precious decorative art to the collar worn by the famous life-saving dog Swansea Jack; and from the hand tools of traditional trades to examples of today's groundbreaking technologies. You will also find a shop and a café in the quayside warehouse, linked to a spectacular new gallery clad in Welsh slate, in which the museum is housed.
• Car parks nearby.
Phone: 01792 638950
www.museumwales.ac.uk

Swansea Grand Theatre. At the heart of the city, this charming theatre presents over five hundred performances a year in all styles of entertainment from comedy to classical music, drama to ballet, opera to the much-loved traditional Christmas pantomime. The Arts Wing hosts exhibitions and the Rooftop Cafe Bar is a dramatic meeting place.

Above left: **Swansea city centre.** Swansea's bustling city centre has numerous restaurants and bars offering world cuisine and fine wines.
Above right: **Swansea Marina.** This sculpture of blind Captain Cat, Dylan Thomas's memorable character from Under Milk Wood, stands on the quayside at Swansea Marina.

• In the main shopping area, conveniently close to train and bus stations and car parks.
Phone: 01792 475715
www.swanseagrand.co.uk

Taliesin Arts Centre. A very popular venue presenting a wide variety of performances and exhibitions, the centre is named after Taliesin, the 6th century Celtic bard. Over the past twenty years, the programme of activities and events has grown to include regular cinema screenings, an average of ten visiting exhibitions per year, and a great variety of live performances from dance and drama to jazz and world music.
• Phone: 01792 602060
www.taliesinartscentre.co.uk

Swansea Museum. This is a traditional museum of local history where you will find display cases filled with fascinating exhibits. There is an Egyptian mummy and a 'Cabinet of Curiosities' packed with the sort of thing that intrigued the Victorians, including a preserved Dodo. A superb collection of toys and games will bring back many memories, and there are exquisite examples of Swansea and Nantgarw pottery.
• Opposite the end of Wind Street and a short walk from the National Waterfront Museum.
Phone: 01792 653763
www.swanseaheritage.net

Dylan Thomas Centre. Born at Cwmdonkin Drive in the Uplands area, the son of an English teacher at Swansea Grammar School, Dylan Thomas was prodigiously talented with words and became the most famous of all Welsh poets working in the English language. The Dylan Thomas Centre has an exhibition about his life and work, and an excellent bookshop-café. Pick up a leaflet for the trail to his birthplace and visit other significant locations including nearby **Cwmdonkin Park** where he played as a child and later found inspiration for poetry.
• Between the National Waterfront Museum and the Sail Bridge. Phone: 01792 463980
www.dylanthomas.com

Swansea Castle. The remains of Swansea Castle are now dwarfed by the modern buildings that surround them, but a fine fortress once dominated the harbour below. The remains of the castle's tower date back to the late 13th century: the distinctive arcaded parapet, added later, is reminiscent of the episcopal palaces at **Lamphey** and **St David's**.

Above: **National Waterfront Museum.** Information technology of the entertaining and visitor-friendly variety is put to helpful use in describing and interpreting the themes explored at Swansea's National Waterfront Museum.

• Near the top of Wind Street, overlooking the city's main shopping area.
www.cadw.wales.gov.uk

Brangwyn Hall. This excellent concert hall, often used for broadcasting and recording, is decorated by a series of enormous and colourful murals depicting scenes from the British Empire. They were originally painted by Sir Frank Brangwyn for the House of Lords, but having been deemed rather too visually prominent for that building they were found an appreciative home here. The Brangwyn Hall is part of Swansea's impressive Civic Centre, built in Art Deco style during the 1930s.
• A short drive or bus ride to the

west of the shopping area, towards the university.
Phone: 01792 635489
www.swansea.gov.uk

Festivals and events

Dylan Thomas Festival.
Beginning on his birthday, the 27th of **October**, and ending on the anniversary of his death, the 9th of **November** – as the autumn nights draw in over the streets of his 'ugly lovely town' – Swansea celebrates the life and work of the city's most famous son. The **Dylan Thomas Centre** and the nearby **Dylan Thomas Theatre** are focal points for a full programme of readings, lectures and celebrations around the city.
• Details from the Dylan

Thomas Centre.
Phone: 01792 463980
www.dylanthomas.com

Swansea's festivals. From
May to **September** during the
Swansea Bay Summer Festival,
the city and its environs are alive
to music and entertainment of all
kinds, including the **Proms
in the Park** concerts, open-air
**Shakespeare at Oystermouth
Castle**, and a host of children's
events. The **National Transport
Festival of Wales** and the
Maritime and Sea Shanty Festival
are part of the fun. The **Swansea
Festival of Music and the Arts**,
held each **October**, is one of
Wales's major regional festivals;
it offers a wealth of classical
music at the highest standards

of performance.
• Details from the Tourist
Information Centre near the
bus station.
www.swanseabayfestival.net

Above left: **Dylan Thomas Centre.**
Visit this exhibition to see how
growing up in Swansea helped
shape the great poet's destiny.
Above right: **Swansea Festival.**
A packed programme of events
each summer includes everything
from colourful carnival processions
to musical and theatrical
performances at the highest level.

Where to eat and stay

Alphabetical listing with contact details of restaurants and accommodation

Angel Inn, Salem
Phone: 01558 823394

Butchers Arms, Llanddarog
Phone: 01267 275330

Cnapan*, Newport
Phone: 01239 820575
www.online-holidays.net/cnapan

Cors*, Laugharne
Phone: 01994 427219

Didier & Stephanie's, Swansea
Phone: 01792 655603

Druidstone*, Haverfordwest
Phone: 01437 781221
www.druidstone.co.uk

Fairyhill*, Gower
Phone: 01792 390139
www.fairyhill.net

Falcon*, Carmarthen
Phone: 01267 237152
www.falconcarmarthen.co.uk

Hanson's, Swansea
Phone: 01792 466200

Hurst House*, Laugharne
Phone: 01994 427417
www.hurst-house.co.uk

King Arthur, Reynoldston
Phone: 01792 390775
www.kingarthurhotel.co.uk

Knights, Mumbles
Phone: 01792 363184

La Braseria, Swansea
Phone: 01792 469683
www.labraseria.com

Lower Haythog Farm*,
Nr Haverfordwest
Phone: 01437 731279
www.lowerhaythogfarm.co.uk

Old Kings Arms*, Pembroke
Phone: 01646 683611
www.oldkingsarmshotel.co.uk

PA's Wine Bar, Mumbles
Phone: 01792 367723
www.paswinebar.co.uk

Refectory at St Davids, St Davids
Phone: 01437 721760
www.refectoryatstdavids.co.uk

St Brides*, Saundersfoot
Phone: 01834 812304
www.stbrideshotel.com

Stone Hall*, Nr Haverfordwest
Phone: 01348 840212
www.stonehall-mansion. co.uk

Tregynon Farmhouse*,
Nr Fishguard
Phone: 07970 627910
www.tregynon-cottages.co.uk

Welcome to Town Inn,
Llanrhidian
Phone: 01792 390015
www.thewelcometotown.co.uk

Yr Hen Dafarn, Llansteffan
Phone: 01267 241656

* Accommodation available

Information and useful websites

Tourist Information Centres throughout Wales have expert and welcoming staff who can offer independent assistance with planning routes, booking accommodation and the search for information on places or events to visit. They are your one-stop shop for holiday and short-break information, late availability and last-minute offers.

For a full list of Tourist Information Centres www.visitwales.com

Tourist Information Centres:
Pembrokeshire T 01834 842402

Carmarthenshire – the Garden of Wales T 01267 231557

Swansea Bay – the Gower Peninsula, Mumbles, Afan and the Vale of Neath T 01792 468321

Useful websites

Castles and heritage:
www.cadw.wales.gov.uk
www.nationaltrust.org.uk
www.bbc.co.uk/wales/history
(BBC Wales)
www.merlinshill.com
www.dylanthomas.org
www.gardenofwales.org.uk
(National Botanic Garden)
www.aberglasney.org

Museums and galleries:
www.museumwales.ac.uk
www.waterfrontmuseum.co.uk

Festivals and events:
www.eisteddfod.org.uk
(the National Eisteddfod of Wales)
www.urdd.org/eisteddfod (Urdd
Youth Eisteddfod)
www.artswales.org.uk
(Arts Council of Wales)
www.thingstodo.org.uk
www.homecomingwales.com

Other websites
www.ccw.gov.uk (National Trails)
www.pembrokeshirecoast.org
(Pembrokeshire Coast
National Park)
www.swansea.gov.uk
www.pembrokeshire.gov.uk
www.carmarthenshire.gov.uk
www.visitwales.com
www.nationalparks.gov.uk
www.wales.gov.uk

How to get here

By car. The UK's road network serves visitors to Wales well, making it easy to get to by car. In the north the A55 coastal Expressway provides a trouble-free, fast route to the north coast.

By train. Wales is easy to get to from all of the UK. From London Paddington there is a service that will take you to Swansea in three hours.

If you are visiting from overseas you will find that there are good links between all major airports and the main rail network. For rail enquiries and booking ring + 44(0) 8457 48 49 50 or visit one of the following websites: www.nationalrail.co.uk, www.thetrainline.com or www.qjump.co.uk

By coach or bus. National Express offers a nationwide service of fast, reliable express coaches. There is a good service from London Victoria coach station to many towns and cities in Wales as well as from many cities and towns in both England and Scotland. For example, the journey time for direct services from Birmingham Digbeth to Carmarthen is around four and a half hours. There are also convenient Flightlink coach services from major airports to destinations in Wales. For information and bookings call + 44 (0) 8705 808080 or go to: www.nationalexpress.co.uk Inside Wales there is an extensive network of regional and local bus services.

By air. There are regular direct flights to Cardiff International Airport from a wide range of destinations, including Amsterdam, Cork, Glasgow, London City, Paris and Prague. Also, Amsterdam, Dublin and Paris act as gateway hubs for European and international flights. For flight information call +44 (0) 1446 711111 email infodesk@cwl.aero or visit www.cial.co.uk London's airports and those at Birmingham and Manchester are all good gateways to Wales. Each has good road and rail connections.

By sea. Three ferry companies operate services between south-west Wales and Ireland. They are:
Irish Ferries.
Rosslare to Pembroke.
Tel: +44 (0) 8705 171717
www.irishferries.com
Stena Line. Rosslare to Fishgard.
Tel: +44 (0) 8705 707070
www.stenaline.co.uk
Swansea-Cork ferries.
Cork to Swansea.
Tel: +44 (0) 1792 456116
www.swanseacorkferries.com

Other ferry ports (along England's south coast and elsewhere) have good cross-country motorway and main road links to Wales. For car travellers arriving on the EuroTunnel service it is motorway all the way from Dover to Wales.

Castles and heritage throughout Wales

Most of the many archaeological sites, castles and historic houses of Wales, and numerous former centres of industry, are in the care of one of two agencies – Cadw or the National Trust. It is said that if a historic property has a roof, then it is likely to be run by the National Trust; otherwise it is probably the responsibility of Cadw. Not an infallible guide, of course, but a helpful start.

Wales has more castles and fortifications for its area than anywhere else in Europe. If you include every earthwork revealed by archaeological surveys and aerial photography, there are more than six hundred sites. Their number and variety reflect the nation's turbulent and fascinating history.

In prehistoric times, life was a constant struggle for survival against the elements and attack by others. The earliest inhabitants of Wales made stone tools and weapons, but their limited building abilities were mainly directed at ceremonial matters and the commemoration of their dead. Though primitive fortifications exist, they are not substantial.

The **Celtic tribes**, who lived throughout what we now call the UK and Ireland before the arrival of the **Romans**, were notoriously warlike. The landscape – especially coastal promontories and hilltops with good views – is peppered with the remains of their substantial forts.

Above: **Chirk Castle.** The last of the castles built by Edward I in his conquest of Wales, Chirk Castle has fantastic gardens and a stunning view over nine counties.

The Romans introduced a sophisticated network of forts, barracks, roads and ports to sustain their legions as they encountered the troublesome tribes of the region they called **Cambria**. Many indigenous **Celts** eventually saw the advantage of adopting Roman ways, and their pragmatic co-operation made possible the governance of this remote extremity of the empire.

When the Romans began pulling out of their distant province of Britannia towards the end of the 4th century, the power vacuum was filled by regional rulers who provided the inspiration for the legendary **King Arthur**, mentioned for the first time in an early Welsh poem and later idealised into a paragon of chivalry.

The Saxons conquered much of what is now England but found Wales and Scotland fiercely resistant. During the 8th century, the eponymous **King Offa of Mercia** ordered the building of his dyke, a low earthwork that marked the western limit of his ambition and recognised the separateness of Wales.

On the Welsh side of **Offa's Dyke**, regional kings and princes consolidated their rule. Their courts were usually peripatetic and their households – families, soldiers, servants, minstrels and poets – moved between several castles. Through war, treaty and marriage their territories began to coalesce into an emerging Welsh nation.

In 1039, **Gruffudd ap Llywelyn** became the first ruler of a united and independent Welsh nation that was organised upon a sophisticated legal and constitutional foundation. But this was not the best timing. Within a couple of decades of the arrival of **William the Conqueror** in 1066, the **Normans** had taken the lands and powers of the Welsh princes in much of south-eastern Wales and were extending their influence and building their solid castles throughout the lowlands.

In 1267, **Llywelyn ap Gruffudd** was recognised by **Henry III as Prince of Wales**, but this harmonious arrangement was also short-lived. The English king **Edward I**, who came to power in 1272, aimed to bring Wales and Scotland fully under his rule. He spent vast sums in building his 'iron ring' of castles around Gwynedd, from where Llywelyn mounted his campaigns to retain

Clockwise from top left:
Gwydir Castle interior and exterior. Regarded as the finest Tudor house in Wales, Gwydir Castle was once the home to Katheryn of Berain, cousin of Elizabeth I.
Caldey Abbey. Caldey has been home to various orders of monks since Celtic times. Today the picturesque monastery overlooks the pretty island cottages, Village Green and Shop.
Tenby Tudor Merchant's House. This late 15th century town house is furnished to recreate the atmosphere of family life in Tudor times.

independence. Having succeeded in securing solid support throughout Wales against overwhelming forces, Llywelyn was eventually ambushed and killed at Cilmeri near Builth Wells in 1282.

Numerous fortified mansions and grand homes in the style of medieval castles have been built in Wales since those distant days of strife, but the pinnacle of castle building for military purposes was in the time of Edward I. The remarkable architecture and ingenuity of four of his castles – **Caernarfon, Conwy, Harlech** and **Beaumaris** – built by Master James of St George, the French genius in such matters, has been recognised in their collective designation as a UNESCO World Heritage Site.

Until the mid-18th century, Wales was a largely rural nation where landowners enjoyed the resources to build fine houses, and agricultural workers and their families lived modestly. The coastline was dotted with small harbours where fishing was the main activity.

The largest structures were the castles, which had long since outlived their purpose, and the great religious buildings, including the ruins of medieval abbeys.

The Industrial Revolution rapidly transformed the working pattern, the economy, the built environment and the social fabric of Wales. Within a few decades,

small towns and villages were transformed into some of the largest concentrations of industry in the world.

Merthyr Tydfil became the world's largest iron-producing centre, making possible the building of the railways. A pall of noxious fumes over **Swansea** and **Llanelli** reflected their specialisation in the smelting of copper, tin and other metals. Large numbers of people flocked to Wales from England and further afield, to provide manpower for the new industries.

The mining of coal in the south Wales Valleys boomed to the point where, by the early 20th century, 250,000 men toiled underground and **Cardiff** became the world's largest coal-exporting port. By this time, the combined population of the mining towns of the south Wales Valleys was equivalent – in number and variety of origin – to that of an additional large city.

Previous page: **Conwy Castle.** The castle's well-preserved walls give visitors the opportunity to walk along the top portions of the castle towers and town walls.
Above left: **Caerphilly Castle.** The castle was a revolutionary masterpiece of 13th century military planning due to its immense size (1.2h) and its large-scale use of water for defence.
Above right: **Menai Bridge.** At the time it was completed, Thomas Telford's bridge was the largest suspension bridge in the world.

The slate quarries of north and mid Wales expanded to meet the demand for roofing material at home, in Europe and in north America. Seaports grew to handle the thriving trade in raw materials and goods – and, as the railway network grew, to serve the passenger traffic to and from Ireland. Manufacturing industry expanded, particularly in south-eastern and north-eastern Wales.

Many of the industrial buildings and structures that made this ferment of activity possible – along with the grand houses built on its wealth – may be visited today. These heritage sites provide a fascinating insight into the way the people of Wales lived and worked in times gone by.

Several sites of the National Museum Wales (please see overleaf) provide especially direct insights into the industries that were so significant in shaping the appearance of the land and the character of the people.

Above: **Basingwerk Abbey.** During the 13th century Anglo-Welsh wars, Basingwerk's sympathies lay with the English. It apparently suffered little, and by the later 15th century had become quite prosperous. It was dissolved in 1536.

Left: **Bodnant Garden.** Spanning some 80 acres, Bodnant Garden is one of the most beautiful gardens in the UK.

Museums and galleries throughout Wales

In addition to the National Museums, you will find that most towns have a museum or heritage centre dedicated to the extraordinary variety of life and culture to be found in this deeply fascinating part of the world.

As befits a nation with such a rich history and well-preserved material heritage, Wales has many excellent museums.

The **National Museum Wales** is a widely dispersed group of leading institutions. The **National Slate Museum** in Llanberis, tells how the quarrymen extracted the versatile building and roofing material from the mountains, and describes their tough lives. The

National Wool Museum in the Teifi valley is the place to try carding and spinning for yourself, and to learn all about wool production and use.

Few museums offer anything quite as dramatic as the underground tour at the **Big Pit National Coal Museum** near Blaenavon. And few put information technology to such

Above left: **Oriel Mostyn Gallery.** The Oriel Mostyn Gallery in Llandudno north Wales is one the UK's premier contemporary, modern and fine art galleries. Above right: **National Museum Cardiff.** The National Museum Cardiff houses one of Europe's finest art collections as well as preserving some of the nation's treasures.

effective use as the **National Waterfront Museum** in Swansea, which tells the story of the people of Wales at work, in industries old and new.

St Fagans National History Museum is one of Europe's very best open-air museums, featuring a wonderful collection of buildings relocated from all over Wales, together with absorbing indoor exhibitions about rural life and folk traditions.

The **National Museum Cardiff** is the nation's storehouse of all that is best in many and varied fields of interest – from archaeology to zoology, decorative arts, fine art, geology, science, technology and many other areas.

In addition to the National Museums, you will find that most towns have a museum or heritage centre dedicated to the extraordinary variety of life and culture to be found in this deeply fascinating part of the world.

Interesting museums include the **Llangollen Motor Museum** and **Pendine Museum of Speed**, the **National Coracle Centre**, which displays coracles from all over the world, the **Rhondda Heritage Park** and the **Blaenavon World Heritage Museum**, a testimony to the pre-eminence of south Wales as the world's major producer of iron and coal in the 19th century.

Wales has a long tradition of artistic expression, which continues today. Many gifted

artists and craftspersons live and work here and their work is sold from galleries and studios across the land. Collections of fine art, from Wales and elsewhere, have been assembled both by the nation and by individual collectors.

Collections of fine art, from Wales and elsewhere, have been assembled both by the nation and by individual collectors.

National Museum Cardiff
displays many treasures including a significant collection of Impressionist works by Renoir, Monet and Cézanne. Eminent Welsh artists also feature, including 18th century landscape pioneers Richard Wilson and Thomas Jones, and 20th century artists Augustus John, Gwen John and Ceri Richards.

The **National Portrait Gallery** in Wales has over 100 portraits from the 19th century collections including works by John Singer Sargent and the Pre-Raphaelites.

The **Turner House Gallery** in Penarth shows fine art of the highest quality.

Above: National Portrait Gallery.
The National Portrait Gallery at Bodelwyddan Castle houses many wonderful portraits from the 19th century.

The westernmost regions of Wales (especially Anglesey, Snowdonia and Pembrokeshire) have inspired many artists. Look out for pleasing depictions of landscape, seascape, the seasons and rural life by Sir Kyffin Williams RA, William Selwyn, Rob Piercy, John Knapp-Fisher, Donald McIntyre and others.

Clusters of high-quality artists' studios may be found at Glynllifon (near Caernarfon), Ruthin, Hay-on-Wye and St Clears.

The biennial **Artes Mundi** competition at the **National Museum Cardiff** features the work of international conceptual artists.

Above left: **St Fagans.**
St Fagans Castle with its splendid Rose Garden is only one of many buildings you can explore in this informative open-air museum. Step back in time as far as the Iron Age and experience how Welsh people once lived and worked.
Above right: **National Waterfront Museum.** At the National Museum Wales's newest attraction you can experience noise, grime, high finance, upheaval, consumerism and opportunity and see how Wales's Industrial Revolution help shape the rest of the world.
Left: **Aberystwyth Arts Centre.**
The award-winning Aberystwyth Arts Centre has a wide-ranging programme of events and activities across all art forms. It is recognised as a national centre for arts development and welcomes over 650,000 visitors a year through their doors.

Festivals and events throughout Wales

There are festivals in Wales for just about every aspect of culture. You will find everything from large national events to local musical and literary festivals, carnivals, regattas and shows that draw the crowds to historic villages, towns and harbours.

You will find everything from large national events to local musical and literary festivals, carnivals, regattas and shows that draw the crowds to historic villages, towns and harbours.

The main tourism season in Wales extends from Easter onwards, through the summer, until the school term begins in early September. Countless events, suitable for all the family, are organised during these months. Many places also provide ample reason to visit throughout the year, by organising activities and entertainment appropriate to autumn, Christmas, and other times.

Above left: **Aberystwyth and Ceredigion County Show.** This County Show is one of many across Wales that promote agriculture and bring together the farming industry and the local community. Shows like these hold a number of events that make great days out for visitors.
Above right: **The Big Cheese, Caerphilly.** This is an annual celebration of local and Welsh heritage, history, culture and entertainment. The festival includes jugglers, fire eaters, living history re-enactments, music, funfair rides and more.

Musical, literary and theatrical enthusiasms feature strongly and you will find performances at every level from professional venue to village hall. The orchestra of **Welsh National Opera** and the **BBC National Orchestra of Wales** appear at spectacular open-air concerts each summer; at Swansea's Proms in the Park, Cardiff Bay and elsewhere.

Musical styles ranging from classical to brass bands, and from jazz to folk and roots music, have strong followings at festivals, halls and clubs across the land. Authentic Welsh folk traditions, including music and dance, are still celebrated, notably in and around Cardiff, at the beginning of May and at Christmas and New Year.

The traditions of the countryside are a recurrent theme, central to the identity of many Welsh people. Despite the demands of the farming life, the seasonal pattern allows time for the agricultural shows at local and national level. The largest of these, the **Royal Welsh Agricultural Show** is held at Builth Wells during **July**, with the **Winter Fair** following at the same venue early in **December**. Smaller shows, to which all are welcome, are organised at county level throughout Wales.

Some of the more vigorous, and occasionally dangerous, traditional sports have disappeared but Wales has made a unique contribution in this area

of endeavour. The little town of **Llanwrtyd Wells** has become famous for its calendar of what can only be described as profoundly wacky challenges, including the **world bog-snorkelling championships**! The latter requires an unusual ability to ignore the cold and unsavoury surroundings, and to navigate in zero visibility, as you swim as rapidly as you can for the finish line.

The largest annual events arrive one after the other during the spring, summer and early autumn. Typically organised by experienced professionals supported by resourceful local committees, they feature big names in their respective fields and provide a visitor experience second-to-none.

Llanwrtyd Wells has become famous for its world bog- snorkelling championships!

Above: **Welsh National Opera at Cardiff Bay.** The Oval Basin at Cardiff Bay hosts fabulous open-air concerts by big names, including Welsh National Opera, as well as being a venue for other events such as Cardiff's International Food and Drink Festival.

The Hay Festival of Literature, held each May, sees world-famous authors, and enthusiastic readers.

The **Hay Festival of Literature**, held each **May**, sees world-famous authors, and enthusiastic readers who appreciate a good book, congregating at the small town of Hay-on-Wye, which has more than 30 bookshops.

Brecon pulsates to the sounds of jazz during **August**, when traditional bands and skilled solo practitioners of the more rarified forms come to town for the **Brecon Jazz Festival**.

Bryn Terfel, the world's leading bass-baritone, invites world-class guests to join him on stage before an enthusiastic home audience at his annual **Faenol Festival** (voted Best Show in Wales) held near Bangor each **August** Bank Holiday.

The Cardiff Festival offers an exciting series of concerts throughout the summer.

The **Cardiff Festival** offers an exciting series of concerts, a multicultural carnival, a harbour festival, food shows, sports competitions and many other events throughout the summer, in the city centre and at Cardiff Bay.

Celebrations of food and produce, including the **Abergavenny Food Festival**, make a point of inviting local companies to provide the best possible food and drink – both home-produced and more exotic.

The largest of Wales's cultural festivals – in fact, one of the largest in Europe, with a daily attendance typically exceeding 20,000 – is the **National Eisteddfod**. This week-long gathering follows a tradition established by Lord Rhys at Cardigan Castle in 1176, whereby poets and musicians (and nowadays many other talented and creative participants) meet in a spirit of friendly competition.

Clockwise from top left:
Hay Literature Festival. This world-renowned literary festival hosts talks and book signings of the biggest names of the time. Authors from around the world come here to promote their new books. A must for book-lovers.
Brecon Jazz Festival. One of the best jazz festivals in Europe and all the tickets to see the big names performing will go fast. Even if you don't have a ticket, you can soak up the Festival's vibrant atmosphere.
Abergavenny Food Festival. Eagerly awaited by foodies, the Abergavenny Food Festival is one of the largest in the UK.

HAY
ON
WYE
BOOKS

JUICE BAR MENU

FRUIT JUICES
INSTANT ENERGY Kiwi Apple Carrot
SUPERJUICE Grapefruit, Orange, Lime
VITAMIN KICK Peach, Apple, Grape
TROPICANA Pineapple, Kiwi, Orange
INCREDIBLE LEMON Apple, Lemon
TUTTI FRUTTI Strawberry Kiwi Apple

VEGETABLE JUICES
WHEATGRASS, CARROT
BEET

FRESH FRUIT & SALAD

The largest of Wales's cultural festivals – in fact, one of the largest in Europe, with a daily attendance typically exceeding 20,000 – is the National Eisteddfod.

Held at the beginning of **August**, the **National Eisteddfod** moves to a different part of Wales each year. The enormous pavilion, venue for competitions and evening concerts, seats some 3,500 people. The surrounding Maes, or campus, has several smaller performance and exhibition spaces and upwards of 300 stands, where most of Wales's cultural and educational organisations are represented.

The central point of the **National Eisteddfod** is that everything happens in the Welsh language. Simultaneous-translation receivers are available at the main entrance and anyone wishing to learn the language will be made welcome at the Learners' Pavilion – there's a hotly contested prize for Welsh Learner of the Year.

The principle of friendly competition has been extended worldwide by the **Llangollen International Musical Eisteddfod**. This captivating multicultural gathering originated in 1947 as a means of bringing together like-

minded people from all over war-ravaged Europe. One of its most moving moments being the first appearance by a choir from Germany in 1949. Performers of appropriately high ability nowadays travel from all over the world to attend in a spirit of shared appreciation.

Little wonder then, that this is the only festival in the world to have been nominated for the Nobel Peace Prize.

Performers of appropriately high ability nowadays travel from all over the world to attend in a spirit of shared appreciation.

Above left: **Royal Welsh Show.** The Royal Welsh Show is one of the most prestigious events of its type in Europe, and brings to together the farming industry and rural community in a celebration of the best of British agriculture with a unique and very special 'Welsh' flavour.

Above right: **Cardiff Festival.** Cardiff Festival is the UK's largest free outdoor festival, and brings colour and cultural vibrancy to the city and the waterfront area of Cardiff Bay.

The Welsh language

The ancient language of Wales is very much alive during the 21st century and is spoken by around half a million people.

Welsh evolved from the Celtic languages spoken throughout Britain at the time of the Roman occupation. These included two distinct forms: the Goidelic group, which produced the Irish, Scots Gaelic and Manx (Isle of Man) languages, and the Brythonic group, from which the Welsh, Cornish and Breton languages emerged.

Welsh is one of Europe's oldest languages and is by far the strongest survivor of all the Celtic tongues. As with all languages, it has over many centuries absorbed words and influences from elsewhere.

There is no compulsion to speak Welsh but many people deeply enjoy doing so. The lyrical nature of the language seems designed to produce pleasingly poetic sounds and opens the door to a treasure trove of culture. Even the smallest attempt at learning the basics will be much appreciated by the people you meet, even if they need to help you a little with some of the pronunciation.

The language is generally phonetic, so that each letter represents only one sound: what is written is what you say. Some of the sounds however differ from English, as follows:

'a' as in 'apple'
'e' as in 'exit'
'i' as in 'ee'
'o' as in office
'u' sounds similar to the 'i' in 'win', but longer
'w' as in 'win' - serves as a vowel
'y' as the 'u' in 'cup', but longer – serves as a vowel
the famous 'll' is akin to the 'tl' sound in the English words 'antler' or 'Bentley'- but you breathe out gently as you say it.
the Welsh 'ch' is similar to that in Johann Sebastian Bach, a highly regarded figure in Wales!
'dd' sounds like the 'th' in then
'th' sounds like the 'th' in thing

Websites
www.bwrdd-yr-iaith.org.uk
(information on the Welsh language)
www.bbc.co.uk/wales/learnwelsh

A few helpful words and phrases

Good morning	Bore da
Good afternoon	Prynhawn da
Goodbye	Hwyl fawr
Good evening	Noswaith dda
Good health!/Cheers	Iechyd da!
Good night	Nos da
How are you?	Sut mae?
Very good	Da iawn
Welcome	Croeso
Welcome to Wales	Croeso i Gymru
fine thanks	iawn diolch
yes	ie
no	na
please	os gwelwch yn dda
Thank you	Diolch
Good	Da
small	bach
big	mawr
where is?	ble mae?
castle	castell
river	afon
food	bwyd
drink	diod
I'd like a pint of...	Hoffwn i beint o...
And a glass of...	a gwydriad o...
Where am I?	Ble ydw i?
I'm lost!	Dwi ar goll!
Where's the nearest cashpoint?	Ble mae'r twll yn y wal agosaf?

Graffeg books

Graffeg publish illustrated books about contemporary life in Wales. Each book is focused on a particular interest: landscapes, food, lifestyle, heritage, architecture, festivals, music, arts, sports and culture. Graffeg books make wonderful guides, travelling companions and gifts.

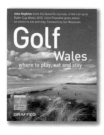

View our catalogue online www.graffeg.com

Visit our website for the latest news and view the Graffeg book list online @ ww.graffeg.com Browse through books online before you order.

Published by Graffeg.
Tel: 029 2037 7312
sales@graffeg.com
www.graffeg.com

About the authors

Written by
David Williams

David Williams is a writer and photographer having a wide-ranging knowledge of the life, culture and history of Wales. He wrote, and supplied images for, the Graffeg books Landscape Wales, About Cardiff and About Wales – and for other titles in this series of pocket guides. He works for numerous book and magazine publishers, broadcasters, tourism authorities and cultural organisations. A graduate of the University of Wales, he is a fluent Welsh speaker.

As a contributor to Photolibrary Wales, his images help to promote Wales worldwide. Having travelled throughout Wales, he is thoroughly familiar with its people and places, and able to offer a balanced perspective on the whole of our compact but enormously fascinating nation.

Foreword by
Siân Lloyd

Originally from Neath, Siân Lloyd attended school in Ystalyfera and studied at the universities of Cardiff and Oxford. She worked as a television presenter with S4C, and as a radio and television journalist, before joining the ITV national weather team. She reports on the environment for ITN, and on travel and environmental matters for national newspapers.

Her wide spectrum of television appearances, as presenter and guest, includes children's programmes, quizzes, chat shows, talent shows, consumer programmes and current-affairs discussions. Her interests include food – cooking it, eating it, and writing and making programmes about it! – mountain walking (from Wales to the Alps), chess, Scrabble, films and theatre.

Index